HOW

![Success Ln / Failure Dr street signs]

By: **Todd Marcell**

Edited By: *Anthony Jones*

Foreword By: *Anthony Jones*

This Book is dedicated to my Dad William "Smitty"
Smith, the coolest person I know

TABLE OF CONTENTS:

Foreword

In his simplistic, straightforward style Todd Marcell delivers the truth to the younger generation that they often don't receive from their peers. In essence, "How to be Cool" speaks to the minds of this generation about how to define "cool" by making wise choices that will serve them well for their entire life. Making wise choices is the opposite of making temporary "uncool" choices, which may get them accepted by others, but will have a detrimental impact upon their lives. As the father of three young black men, he is a trusted resource for advice on how teenagers and young people should handle all of the challenges that they are faced with today.

The goal is to get you as young people to think long-term and not so much in the short-term, which is something that adults struggle with also. For example, you may get a tattoo because you think it's cool. Five years later you may look at that same tattoo and think "I should've gotten something else, I should've gotten the tattoo somewhere else, or maybe I shouldn't have gotten it all!" So now you have a regret, because you've changed your mind about something you once felt passionate about. The good thing about this particular decision is that you can *undo* it; it can be covered, or you can go through a laser removal process. However, this comes with a cost. A cost that can range anywhere from hundreds to thousands of dollars. In life when you make temporary or bad decisions, without thinking about the long-term consequences, there is ALWAYS a cost and every decision can't be undone like a tattoo. If you make the decision to commit a crime you can't *undo* the time that is wasted in jail, or worse if you kill someone you can't bring that person back to life or *undo* the pain that is caused to that family.

Young people you should define "coolness" on your own terms, because if it's defined by somebody else's terms then it is also defined by someone else's expectations. Any time in life that you are defined by someone else's expectations that makes you a slave to that particular person or the "crowd". A person whose life is defined by the expectations of others never truly understands the freedom of being themselves or being *true* to themselves, for that matter. The "crowd" most often will sway you away from making the right choice. Although you may have the desire to do the right thing, fitting in with the crowd may cause you to do the opposite. Therefore "How to Be Cool" is so important because it encourages you to not fit in with the crowd and the benefits you can experience from being your own person.

This book as opposed to many others speaks to teens about how they can be proactive about their own lives. There are many books on the shelves that speaks to us as parents and adults about how to solve some of the crises like: juvenile delinquency, lack of motivation for school, making bad decisions. However, not many speak directly to you all as the new generation, which is most important because we as adults want to foster independence amongst you. In other words we want you to GROW UP and stand on your OWN TWO FEET. You've probably heard it like this from your parents: "Get a job!", "Get out of my house!", "You think I'm made of money?!", and "You don't pay for any groceries stop eating up all of the food!" Basically, the reason we as parents say all of these things is because we want you to understand what it is to be grown and not be dependent upon us one day. You have the ability right now to take advantage of the opportunities before you and create the life that you envision for yourselves.

The power is in your hands young people!
As Mr. Marcell says "The time is now - plan, strive, become!"

Intro: Finding You

What does it mean to be cool? You think it's all about chilling, going with the flow, being laid back, letting things come to you, no that is not it. Being cool is about going after your dreams, succeeding and doing things the right way. It's about holding yourself to a higher standard. Material things don't make you cool; they may make you *look* cool but underneath the surface cool comes from within. There are plenty of people that drive the hot cars, have tons of money, plenty of women, but really, it's just a mirage to hide behind their low self-esteem. They use those things to try to fill a void that's left from not being themselves. Would you rather have all the fixings and be lame? Not me I would rather have all the fixings and my life together. The cool part is that you can have that by
being real with yourself and everyone you meet. It all starts with respect; treat

everyone good like you would want to be treated and you will find favor in whatever you choose. Be a "stand-up" guy and handle your responsibilities. Make good on your promises, meaning keep your word and strive to do things to the best of your ability and that is how you become cool.

"Man can starve from a lack of self-realization as much as… from a lack of bread." – Richard Wright, Native Son, 1940

Chapter 1: Finding Self

Who are you? I know you ask that question to yourself a million times. Deep down inside you know who you are If you have not found yourself yet it is not too late. Drop whatever you're doing and search for it! Do you ever feel like you make choices for yourself depending on what people think about you or how people see you? Well then you are not being yourself, everyone you look up to, it is some reason you look up to him or her. You see the same drive & vision similar to yours inside that person. Yet in still that person is different from everyone else, that is because you may have the same make up or characteristics but no matter how hard you try you cannot be like that person. God MADE everyone different and he made you different, there is something that you do or a quality that you have that no one on earth can imitate. Every artist, every teacher, every talent they possess; no one can do it but them. That is the first thing you need to find out about yourself. What motivates me? What music do I find myself listening to? Who do I admire? Find out that small detail in you that makes you act or behave a certain way that is you being yourself. This is the way God made you and you cannot change it. That does not mean you have to have this nasty attitude or arrogance about yourself that nobody wants to fool with. It means I am confident in whom I am and the person I will become. "So what if I like something different, it's what I like and that's all that matters". One thing I noticed about life is that people will respect you more when you are open & honest about yourself, rather than being someone you're not. Once you find out who you are then you can start to mold yourself into the person you would like to become. Being yourself means you are not bound by limits, you are free to choose whatever. In addition, whatever it is you choose you do not worry about what people think about you. That is why many people don't pursue their dreams or don't finish them and they end up making the wrong choice because they chose the choice of bondage, being held down by someone else's wishes for them. You are bound because you are afraid to let go or make your own choice. Whatever you choose let it be because you want it not because others said you would look or do better doing something else, do it because you know in your heart it is the right thing to do. The heart never lies; that is what God looks at. "Where your heart lies that is where your treasure will be also"(Matthew 6:21). When you achieve something you felt in your heart was right no matter the outcome of the situation you are okay with the results. Hit or miss, you can identify the error and do better the next time. When you do something because someone else does it or try to prove a point to someone then that is what we call "flexing", or not being real. Do not ruin your life being a faker; listening to others best interest about your life. Once you find yourself and decide to be yourself now you can build on that confidence, which will lead us into chapter 2.

"I do not care so much what I am to others as I care what I am to myself."

— Michel de Montaigne

Chapter 2: Confidence

What is confidence?
Confidence is being proud of what you are and not being able to be moved, meaning you stand firm in your beliefs and who you are. It's like when you step into a place or walk with that "swagger" you have this aroma like this is who I am and no one can take that away from me. That is how you earn respect. People respect a person when they are true to themselves. Nobody wants to be around a faker or flexor meaning someone who tries to be something they are not or someone who does things they would not normally do to try to show off. A true person can see right through that. How many times have you seen someone in school or on the streets make a complete fool of themselves, because they were afraid that if they were to show their true identity then no one would want to hang

around them or think they are lame. When you keep it real and be confident in whom you are, you do not care what people think about you. Take Kanye west or Kendrick Lamar for example those guys be on some other stuff but they are confident in their art so everything they breathe on becomes a masterpiece. You have one ultimate

goal every day and that is to be yourself so you can tread your own path. When you find that confidence, it shows in everything you do and with faith, you can achieve it no matter what the odds. Be careful not to confuse faith and confidence although they go hand in hand. Faith is the vision that one has set forth to accomplish whatever it is they try to do and confidence is the belief that I can do it. Confidence believes whatever you choose is the right choice, because you have faith in that choice and that choice will get you one step closer to where you want to be. In addition, it will make you become a better and more complete person. Choosing what you will wear or what college you are planning attend or what career path you choose your confidence plays a big part.

"We are stronger when we listen, and smarter when we share."
— Rania Al-Abdullah

Chapter 3: Communication

Communication is the key if you want to eliminate or avoid the mistakes made by other people so you do not go down that same road and to get insight on different things going on in your life. Honestly if I had communicated to someone about obstacles I faced in my life; my life would have it would took a different turn, one for the better. The first step is wanting to communicate. I used to try to figure out problems or situations on my own, but leaning on your own understanding is not a cool choice not saying that you are not capable of making the right decision, but it may not be the right choice to apply to that situation at that time. You want to choose the wise choice and the wise choice is always the right choice. You need to find someone mostly older or wiser who you feel comfortable talking with. Someone who will not judge you or your situation and seek to communicate with them, you would be surprised to know that they would love to share some knowledge with you. In the

Chinese culture, older are revered. In the western culture older people are forgotten about or treated as if they are of no value anymore. In the Chinese culture, the grandfather or older teacher is the wise person everyone goes to for advice. It does not matter who it is, but make sure they are someone who you know has good insight or has progressed in their lives. If you cannot find anyone at the end of my book I will leave my address and you can write or e-mail me whenever you like. When you have situations or questions about life talking to an elderly or more mature person is very valuable because 9 times out of 10 they have been through that same situation and they can also give you insight on things that you probably would have not thought about on your own because of lack of experience. Pray about the situation also. You can go to God with anything because the Bible says in Proverbs 3:5 "In all your ways acknowledge him and he shall direct your paths".

Also when you communicate with someone it opens you up to receive instruction and heals whatever you are going though. So if you want to be wiser in your decisions or life you will have to communicate. Don't keep things bottled up It's unhealthy and It's unwise. Everybody who is in their career had a mentor to get some advice from. Getting advice does not make you less of a person but more of a person because you are taking heed to warnings. Think about it for a second, the outcome would have been different on some of those decisions if you would have sought some advice, I guarantee.

"The more you know the more you grow"--
Life

Chapter 4: Educate Your Self

Education is the key. This is probably the most important chapter in this book. My brothers and sisters, first let me tell you what great opportunity you have to get an education. Do you not know people died to get an education? People during slavery and the Civil Rights Movement fought their whole lives so you could get an education. The slave masters knew that if you could read, then you could educate yourself and break all the chains, stereotypes, and misconceptions about yourself. What will you do without an education? Work hard all your life. You do not want to work hard it is about working smart. Why forgo your talent, dreams and abilities to end up working a third of your life just to make ends meet.

Meaning you will have no opportunity to do any additional activities like, plan, invest, vacation etc. You are going to be limited to a certain number of professions, yea you can have a trade or a business but if you do not have any education how are you going to market that trade or run that business.

You may say "I will get someone else to run my business. Then him or her will run you out of business because they will steal so much of your money that your business will go bankrupt eventually. That is why I do not understand why people drop out of school; you are making it 10 times harder for yourself. Getting an education is cool, not getting one is not so cool. I never understood why people choose to skip school and not do their work but yet still want a successful life. The world does not work like that you have to put something in to get something out, you cannot get something from nothing. I would rather be in school learning something, laying a foundation for my future. I'll tell you what after you decide that you want to get some business about yourself and you go do what it takes, go back to the hood about 7 or 8 years from now some of the same people who chose to forgo their education, will still be in the same spot I guarantee. Your favorite rappers, actors, and entertainers them people aren't ignorant, meaning lack of knowledge. You may think that flossing and stunting is all they do but you are fooled. Those "cats" are smart! Rapping is just 10% of the artist the rest is business you have to know your audience, competition, and know how to read those contracts or you gone end up like many artists, broke. Behind closed doors, them people are studying their craft as if they are going to take the S.A.T. It does not matter if you are not smart in a certain area, become smart in that area you want to pursue; this is education. Become an expert in the area of your choice then you can hire people to handle the other things. Get an education so when you have kids you will be able to help them. For instance , if you only have an elementary school education, how are you going to teach them about anything on a higher level? You can only teach someone what you know. No matter what you do educate yourself in order to be successful. If you don't get anything from this book get this; Education is your ONLY WAY OUT of your current situation.   Think about it, if you are a ballplayer in any particular sport you still have to go to college to continue your sport. If you aspire to be a musician, you still need to learn how to read and write. No matter what you do you're going to have to get an Education. An Education will take you places, let me break it down for you. No matter how they talk about your school is failing, your school is this, your school is that, it's up to you to make the grades. Here's how it works; it does not matter if you are not naturally book smart, meaning some people have the ability to make schoolwork easy for them, but the other majority of us have to apply ourselves. That means you need to study, do your work, turn it in and make good test scores. So if you need to get a tutor or get extra help then that's what you have to do, because once you understand the lesson, then you will make good grades on your test, homework, schoolwork or what have you. Then that will transfer into making good grades on your report card, which will in turn give you a good GPA. Then you will be able to get into a good college wherever you wish to go. Then if you apply those same work ethics, then you will get more than good enough grades and you will be able to graduate with a degree. After that you can get the career you wish and "bam" you made your path successful and you made it out of your current situation. Now you can reach back take care of your parents or do whatever you want because you will have the means to do so. No one can take knowledge away from you the more you know the more you grow.

Chapter 5: Decisions

"Decisions, decisions to make", this was a song by ATL's own conscience rap group Goodie Mob. The song was about the decisions that we make will either make you or break you. I know people come up with all kind of clichés about how to make a sound decision; well one thing I know is, it is either a bad or a good decision. Every decision that you make has different consequences but every decision you make affects others besides yourself. If you make a bad decision, you may hinder your own plans or not be in position to help others in the future. Making the right decision will steer you away from those pitfalls and future problems. Let me tell you the importance of making the right decision. Making the right decision decreases your stress level because you will not have to worry about that decision coming back to haunt you later in life and it will come back to haunt you. The day you come out of your mother's womb, you have a record. It's up to you to keep it clean. Your record travels with you until the day you leave this earth. So if you do something foolish that bad decision can leave a permanent stain on your record and it could hold you back from certain opportunities. One thing is for sure if you have made a bad decision, you don't always get a chance to turn it around. If you would made the right decision first then you will not have to worry about correcting anything. Make decisions that will move you ahead, not set you back. To know the difference between a bad decision and a good decision listen to your instinct aka sprit. Your spirit is that gut feeling or inner voice in you. Your spirit lets you know that a bad decision is not right. But we all going to make bad decisions, just try to make sure they are less costly as possible. Do not make decisions on impulse or limited knowledge about the situation. A good decision has weeds out negative consequences of the choice. For example, Let's say you have this friend who just got his driver's license and he is known to dabble in drugs. So he swings by your crib and gets you to go for a ride. Knowing that there is a good chance he could be riding dirty, are you going to ride with him? If you get pulled over and he has some drugs in the car or on his possession how do you know if he is going to claim them or blame you? Either way, you are now an accessory or guilty by association. So if you are not sure of a situation then get more info on it and make your decision then; not because you think so, you need to know so. We all make bad decisions, but know your facts and go with the decision that you think will progress you legitimately.

Chapter 6: The Seed

Now that you have determined that you want a prosperous life, we have to sow a seed, meaning you have to set up a plan to get you there, and take the first step. The first step is the seed that puts your plan in motion. Right now, you can write your own destiny. Don't you know you can be anything you want to be. That is guaranteed this is not a mistake. I REPEAT YOU CAN BE ANYTHING YOU WANT TO BE, as long as you follow your plan. God has given you the desire, the vision, the dream, the talent, the skill. First, let us start with what you want to do. Listen to what's in your spirit. What is that feeling you get when you close your eyes and dream? What is that thought in the back of your head you keep thinking about repeatedly? What is that thing you love so much you would do it for free? What is that burning desire that will not go away? Whatever it is, educate yourself on it, become a student of it. There are millions of books and publications on what you want to become, if you cannot find any luck in the book store then try the library or internet and all this information is for free. But whatever it is start now, don't let another day go by without planning your future. Going back to communication, find someone in that field or area you are pursuing and read up on them. Learn from them and if possible find somewhere they are speaking at and attend. Now you have to sketch a plan. Put something in writing start at the smallest point possible, meaning what can you do now that can get you started on your future. Take gradual steps, try to learn it all. I know when you get started it is going to be exciting. But take your time and get knowledge step by step, so when you get your opportunity you will be fully prepared.

OUTRO

The bottom line young brothers is to take advantage of the opportunity at hand! Do not settle for less and be all you can be! You are going to have some haters, but when they hate you that means you are doing something right, and they are trying to pull you down. They know if you go the distance, you will achieve it. Things are going to get bleak sometimes but if you are true to yourself and your mission God tells us that if you take a step out on faith He will walk with you. He just wants you to try to take a swing at your dreams and goals. Keep your eyes on the prize and never give up because when you give up they (haters) win and if they win nobody truly wins. Go ahead, get that paper and when you make it in whatever you choose, you will look back and be proud that you chartered the course and got what's yours and didn't give up and I'm telling you it is

a feeling like no other and that's real talk.
So being cool isn't so bad after all uh.

CONTACT INFO
Write me below @

Todd Marcell
753 Winbrook Dr
Mcdonough,Ga 30253

E-Mail: toddmarcell77@gmail.com

Facebook: learnhowtobecoolbook

Facebook: Author Todd Marcell

Instagram: howtobecoolbook

Website: toddmarcell.com

List of Careers

A-D

- <u>Accountant</u>
- <u>Actuary</u>
- <u>Advertising Managers and Promotions Managers</u>
- <u>Advertising Sales Agent</u>
- <u>Aircraft Mechanic</u>
- <u>Airline Pilot</u>
- <u>Airport Security Screener</u>
- <u>Airline Reservations Agent</u>
- <u>Air Traffic Controller</u>
- <u>Architect</u>
- <u>Auto Mechanic</u>
- <u>Bank Teller</u>
- <u>Bartender</u>
- <u>Biological Technician</u>
- <u>Biomedical Engineer</u>
- <u>Bookkeeping, Accounting, and Auditing Clerks</u>
- <u>Brick Mason</u>
- <u>Budget Analyst</u>
- <u>Cardiovascular Technologist</u>
- <u>Cashier</u>
- <u>Chef</u>
- <u>Chief Executive Officer (CEO)</u>
- <u>Chemical Technician</u>
- <u>Childcare Worker</u>
- <u>Chiropractor</u>
- <u>Claims Adjuster, Appraiser, Examiner, and Investigator</u>
- <u>Compensation and Benefits Manager</u>
- <u>Computer Programmer</u>
- <u>Computer Systems Analyst</u>

- Construction Laborer
- Consultant
- Cook
- Correctional Officer
- Court Reporter
- Curator
- Customer Service Representative
- Database Administrator
- Dental Hygienist
- Dentist
- Derrick Operator
- Diagnostic Medical Sonographer
- Director
- Dietitian/Nutritionist
- Doctor

E - L

- Editor
- Electrician
- EMTs and Paramedics
- English as a Second Language (ESL) Teacher
- Epidemiologist

- Event/Meeting Planner
- Fashion Designer
- Financial Advisor
- Financial Manager
- Financial Services Sales
- Firefighter
- Fitness Trainer
- Flight Attendant
- Funeral Director
- Fundraiser
- Judge
- Glazier

- Grant Writer
- Graphic Designer
- Guidance Counselor
- Hairdressers, Hairstylists, and Cosmetologists
- Health Educator
- Human Resources Assistant
- Human Resources Manager
- Home Health Aide
- Housekeeper
- Industrial Designer
- Industrial Production Manager
- Insurance Underwriter
- Interior Designer
- Interpreter and Translator
- Janitor
- Lawyer
- Librarian
- Library Assistant/Technician
- Licensed Practical Nurse
- Loan Officer
- Lodging Manager

M - P

- Manicurist
- Manufacturing Sales Representative
- Market Research Analyst
- Marriage and Family Therapist
- Massage Therapist
- Mechanical Engineer
- Medical Assistant
- Medical Laboratory Technician
- Model
- Nurse Practitioner
- Nursing Assistant
- Occupational Therapist

- Occupational Therapy Assistant
- Painter
- Paralegal and Legal Assistant
- Personal Trainer
- Pharmacist
- Pharmacy Technician
- Physician Assistant
- Photographer
- Physical Therapist
- Physical Therapy Assistant
- Plumber
- Police Officer
- Postal Service Worker
- Producer
- Psychiatric Aide
- Public Relations Specialist
- Purchasing Manager

R- Z

- Receptionist
- Registered Nurse
- Retail Salesperson
- Retail Supervisor
- Roofer
- Secretary / Administrative Assistant
- Security Guard
- Ski Instructor
- Social Media Manager
- Social Worker
- Software Developer
- Special Education Teacher

- Subway Operator
- Taxi Driver
- Teacher

- Teacher Assistant
- Technical Writer
- Training and Development Manager
- Travel Agent
- Veterinarian
- Veterinary Technician
- Waiter/Waitress
- Web Developer
- Writer